the dimensions of design

design
Ken Cato
pre-press
Mission Productions Limited
printing
Everbest Printing Co. Ltd., Hong Kong/China
©
The Images Publishing Group Pty Ltd
2002

ISBN 1 87690 773 8
Reference number 454

The Images Publishing Group Pty Ltd
Images House
6 Bastow Place
Mulgrave
Victoria 3170
Australia

telephone
(613) 9561 5544
facsimile
(613) 9561 4860
e-mail
books@images.com.au
internet
www.imagespublishinggroup.com

the dimensions of design | **Ken Cato**

# images

A sincere thank you. There are so many people to be acknowledged and thanked. Although my name is on the door it is those who have worked with me throughout the years who deserve much of the credit for the company's success. So much of it has come from working with people who share common goals, the pursuit of excellence, love of design and the profound realisation that good design improves the quality of our lives. Their talent, energy and dedication are the vital ingredients in both the growth of the company and the continuing search for higher standards. The work contained in this book is not the work of one person, it is the accumulated achievement of the people known as Cato Partners and it is them I thank from the bottom of my heart for their talent and support for making the company what it is today.
Ken Cato

| | |
|---|---|
| 6 | Introduction |
| 8 | Ken Cato, An Education in Design |
| 10 | Illustrating the first dimension |
| 40 | Considering the second dimension |
| 60 | Examining the third dimension |
| 102 | Within the fourth dimension |

In viewing this book of Cato's work, the reader will be aware of an irony at play. The Cato philosophy involves an understanding of the dimensions in which all communication works – the elements in which we all see, feel and understand our world. Print is only one of the dimensions through which design communicates, yet it is through print that the philosophy is here being exemplified, consequently there is a need for a few guidelines when viewing the work. Designers are aware that the visual elements should speak for themselves, without lengthy justifications. The more design needs explanations, context and verbiage to justify its presence, the less likely it is that the design is fully communicating in all spheres.

No matter how much is talked and written about the various sub-levels of the effect of design, its visual impact is the first and most immediate part of its ongoing communication. Yet context and philosophy remain important to the art of design and its ultimate goal, which is constant communication between all parties involved. The Cato philosophy understands design as multidimensional, a means of communicating through all the varying levels in which we experience our world. The trademark, sometimes referred to by other designers as the logo, or the marque, occupies only one of the four major dimensions through which we receive messages. This is not to say that Cato sees communication in the hierarchical way of good better and best, with the first dimension being only surface, and the others representing true depth. Designers have, however, become hooked on the notion that the trademark is the apotheosis of communication in the visual sphere – a view from which Cato differs markedly.

One-dimensional thinking is not part of the Cato philosophy, consequently one-dimensional design is, to Cato, thinking in a space that is now antiquated, and through which he has travelled to the other dimensions. Cato communicates through this multidimensional world, one that has only recently opened up to designers, allowing the broadest and more intelligent thinkers new fields for their conversations in design. The depth and breadth that this thinking allows gives Cato the scope with which to communicate at every level, choosing the right voice for the most effective language. While the one-dimensional trademark may be the best solution to a particular problem, two-dimensional print work, such as this book, can be equally important, as can the three-dimensional work with packaging, sculpture and all the objects we can feel, hold and touch.

Cato moves effortlessly into the fourth dimension as well – a new dimension for designers but as old as the earth itself. Here he explores sounds, technology, space and time, because in Cato's philosophy, there are no limits to the way communication flows.
The broader and more sophisticated thinking Cato employs, allows those taking part in the conversation using design as the language to realise that the deeper the message goes, the stronger it is felt and remembered. A memorable trademark will communicate instantly. Broader Visual Language, that which Cato employs, will communicate both instantly and continuously, creating an individual space through which a company or organisation can move yet still keep its core message at the forefront of the conversation. This book has not been designed to layer messages as such, but it is an attempt to show the multiplicity of ways Cato enables communication.

The Cato philosophy is not about just one way of thinking, or one set of specialisations. It is about the most effective and ongoing dialogue between groups of people who are constantly assailed by the instant, by immediate gratification and by, unfortunately, messages that are both inarticulate and strident. Cato logically, and methodically, creates words and sentences in the visual arena that resonate with both the immediate and the lasting. In this way, the messages reach further and deeper, adding to the conversation, rather than joining in the indescribable din that skims the surface of what can only be described as passing chatter.

Ken Cato is logical, intuitive, intelligent and, above all, a teacher. Throughout his career, indeed his life as a designer, he has taught the art of seeing the obvious, of visually simplifying often dense and complex messages of logical thinking brought from the brain to the eye. Cato practices design in partnership with colleagues, both business and professional, and these partnerships are to him the basis of design's most important element, the idea. The idea comes from understanding the needs and minds of others, and harnessing their, and his, skills and knowledge to produce work that above all is effective. He will argue, against the odds, that design is a simple process, constantly underpinned by understanding, by skill, and by the intelligence of logical thinking, to bring about a desirable end to often complex problems. Space is an issue with him. The space in which we live, the space in which design's messages will speak, the three-dimensional, and often four- or five-dimensional space in which he works. The space of which he speaks is limited.

Already crowded, already noisy, and fiercely busy with messages and scribbles that can be strident, confused, bossy or just plain ugly, Cato doesn't speak in subjective terms of beauty or ugliness. He speaks of function, of solutions, of the process. Design has to work, to fulfil a function, to add a value and communicate a message hitherto unknown, dated, or simply inappropriate. The messages often cross cultural and aesthetic boundaries, but are governed and articulated as a coherent whole by design. It unites, by a matrix of thought and intuition, a concept so inherent as to be sometimes indescribable in any other form but the visual. Starting his company in the 70s, within a few years approaches were already being made from the international arena, and by the end of that decade he had worked in more than 20 countries; the list now includes more than 30. It is hard to pinpoint when his worldwide reputation began to coalesce, but somewhere in the early 70s his work attracted the regular attention of international design journals, and clients. He emerged as a front-runner of a new generation of Australian designers, those who looked beyond their own country while never losing its inspiration.

Previously any number of others from afar had joined the queue in Australia, branding the big corporations and imposing a global, rather than truly international, style on work that didn't necessarily last the distance. Cato was instrumental in changing the view that designers need only one cultural context, showing through his work that each and every context in which messages are written is important. By the late 80s and early 90s, the Cato name was well known, and indeed he had worked successfully in countries throughout the world as diverse as it was possible to be. There is nothing parochial about Cato. He now commands, at this point in his career, a reputation supported by solid foundations, which allows thousands of students to gather annually in Melbourne to listen to and learn from, almost every important designer and communicator from a vast array of disciplines and countries. His awards are innumerable, as is the list of organisations of which he is a respected member. Cato remains, however, an essential designer, and a teacher in every sphere in which he works.

# Illustrating the first dimension

Symbols designed as part of corporate identity programmes for financial institutions: Suncorp Metway, Macquarie Bank, GiroPost and Bank Direct

Opposite page: Commonwealth Bank and BankWest

**Commonwealth** Bank
Visual Standards Manual

BANK OF WESTERN AUSTRALIA LTD · PERTH

**BankWest**

MELBOURNE
1996

The Olympic flame was the inspiration behind the symbol and graphics system for the 1996 Melbourne Olympic Bid

Symbol from a corporate identity programme for Infratil, a New Zealand-based management and investment corporation

Symbols from corporate identity programmes for Tasman Paper Recyclers, The John Truscott Foundation, and Metasource, a sustainable energy resource company

Opposite page: Symbols from corporate identity programmes for C&T high-speed telecommunications networks, Energex, Sydney Breast Cancer Institute, The Australian Cricketers Associations, Australia's Best Cars, The Australian Centre for American Studies, Kiboodle, an e-procurement company, ScreenSound Australia and Sydney Airport

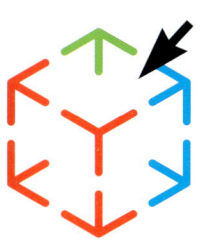

Symbols from corporate identity programmes for Grace Bros department stores, Poppy cosmetics and Primrose Textiles

Opposite page: Symbols from a corporate identity programme for New Zealand's leading wholesale supermarket, The Supply Chain

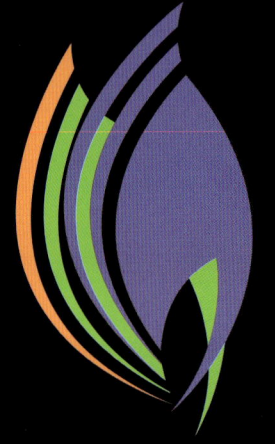

Symbols from corporate identity programmes for the Melbourne Major Events Corporation, Hamburg Airport, Oasis gaming venues, Fashion Bytes, a colour forecasting consultant, Powerco, a New Zealand gas and electricity corporation, and Sorrett publishing

Opposite page: Symbols for Westar, a gas distribution company, and Kinetic Energy

Following pages: Symbols from corporate identity programmes for IAG Insurance Australia Group, Australian Academy of Design, Snowy Mountains Hydro Electric Scheme, Addit Australia, Golf Resorts International, Gloweave, My Future, Victorian Arts Centre, Melbourne International Festival, Royal Guide Dogs Associations of Australia, and the Black Dog Foundation

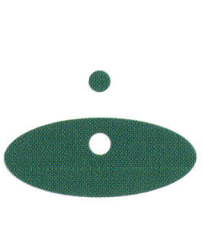

Numerous sub-brand symbols for retirement villages were developed as part of a corporate identity programme for Primelife Corporation, Australia

The symbol from a corporate identity programme for Gardener Press had obvious origins. By taking license with the spelling and meaning of the name, we were able to graphically demonstrate the nature of the business and the quality of the product

The artistic styles of many different cultures provided a rich source of information in the development of symbols that formed the identity for multicultural arts programme Kulcha

A symbol and identity system for the
Australian National University's Centre for the Mind

In the years leading up to the Sydney 2000 Olympic Games, the Darling Harbour Authority held a series of vibrant, outdoor festivals. In developing identities for two of these, the symbol design and graphics were influenced by the names of the festivals, which were all derived from the concept of light

The modular square symbol from the corporate identity programme for Cest La Vie, a Japanese development and building corporation, underpinned the concept of a Broader Visual Language. Opportunities for enhanced communications created the need for constant change to the master symbol to reflect building forms and their architectural characteristics

The ancient Chinese Tangram provided the relationship of each building's form (the square) to the rearranged components which represent the people who inhabited the structures

The C'est La Vision sub-brand symbol was a natural extension of the main company identity. The extensive product range included print and manufactured items related to lifestyle

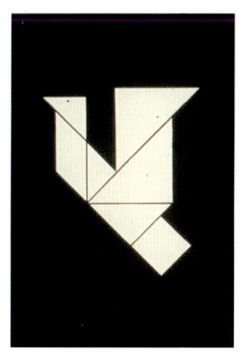
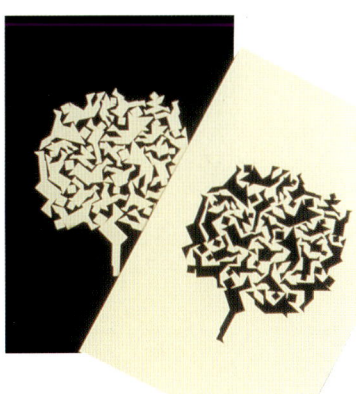

Australia's international airline, Qantas, has a symbol that's well-recognised the world over. Aerial views of the Australian landscape became the basis of a Broader Visual Language that could be translated across a diverse range of applications

# Guidelines for the use of the Qantas corporate identity

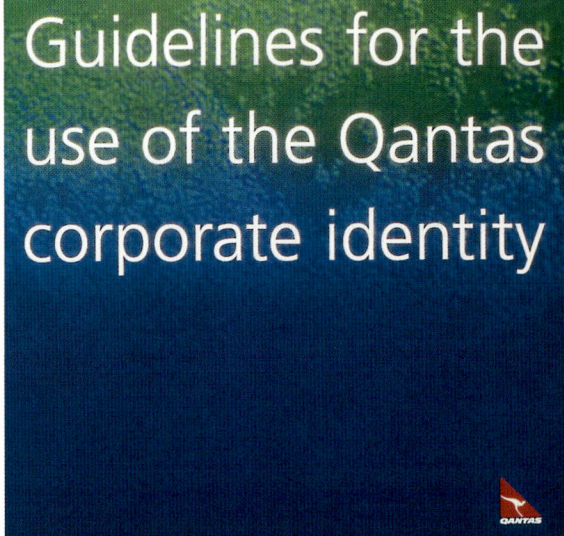

Guidelines were produced to ensure the continuity and integrity of the Broader Visual Language

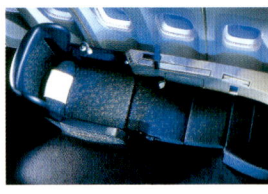

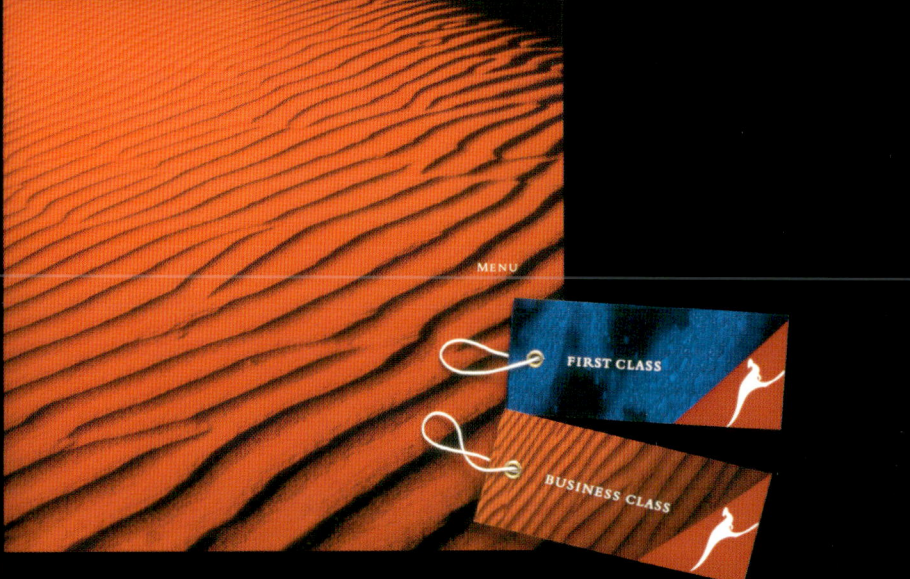

The Australian landscape provided one theme to link all the components that determined the selection of building materials as well as the creation of all graphic elements

The name Members Equity provided an ideal way to create a close visual link with this virtual bank's customers by creating a symbol that utilised the letters m and e. The identity programme allowed an extended visual language to be developed for online communication and also provided the opportunity to identify products and services

Opposite page: The illuminated power grid of a city inspired the symbol and identity programme for Energy Australia. The programme encouraged the trademark characteristics to be used. Ultimately this became more identifiable than the trademark itself

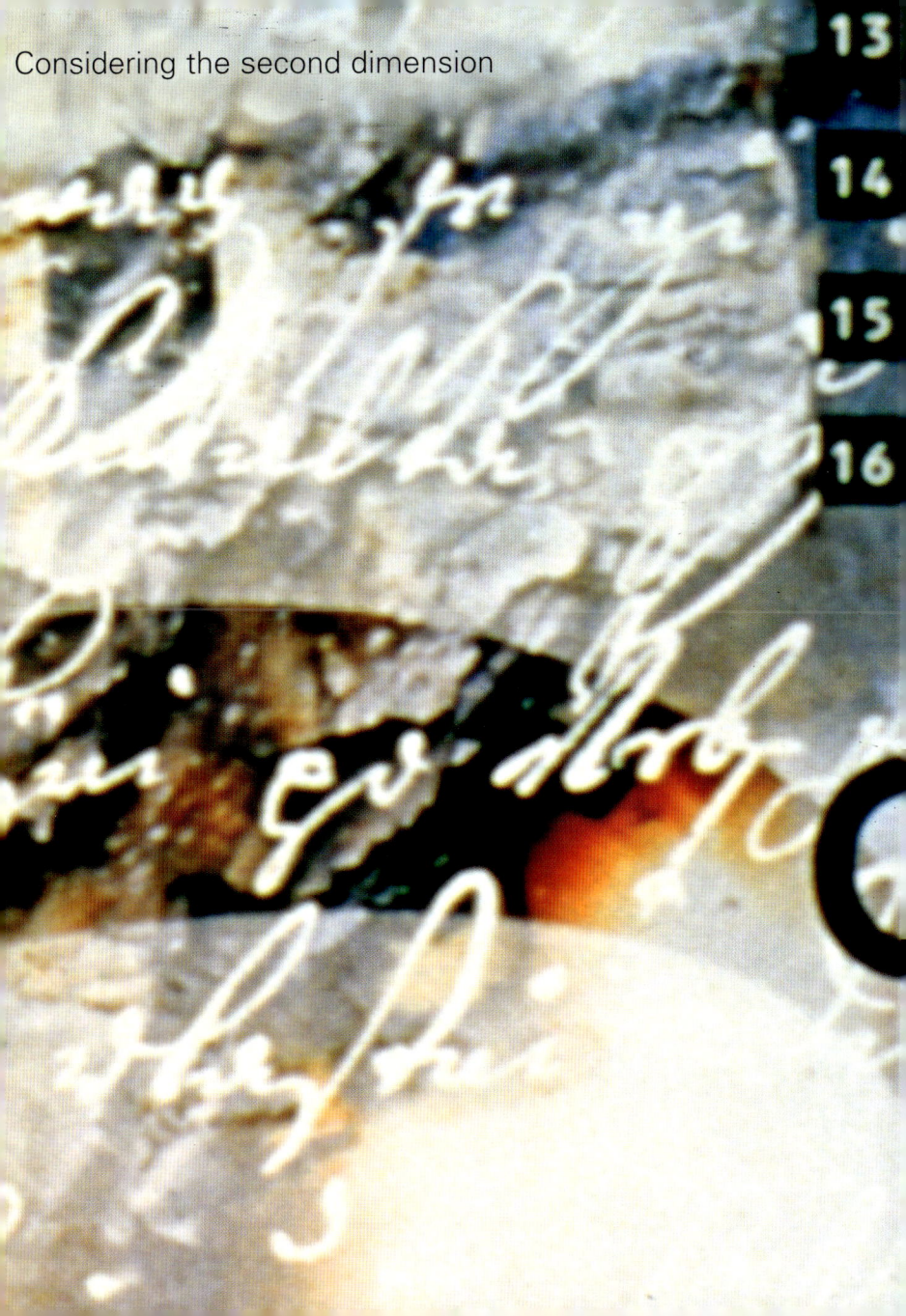

Considering the second dimension

Book covers and editorial spreads from the *Australian Commercial and Magazine Photographers* annuals

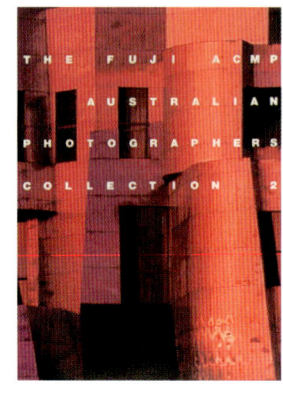

# THE AUSTRALIAN PHOTOGRAPHERS' COLLECTION 1

A promotional calendar designed for Eurasia Press Singapore

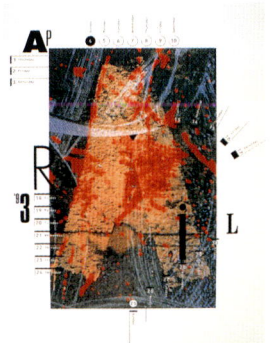

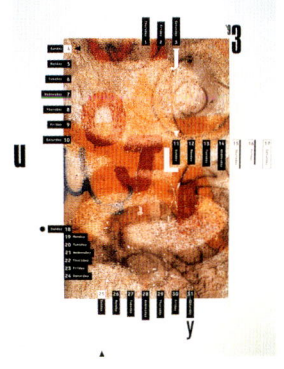

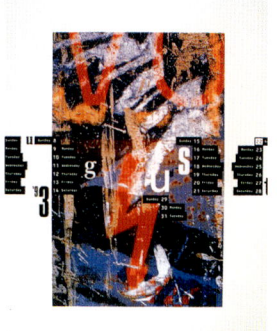

Opposite page: The second edition of 'First Choice' is a volume that gives the world's leading designers the opportunity to select their best work and to provide the criteria for their choices

'Hindsight' is a collection of thoughts and comments from prominent international designers. The book provides personalised answers to the most frequently asked questions of students and followers of design

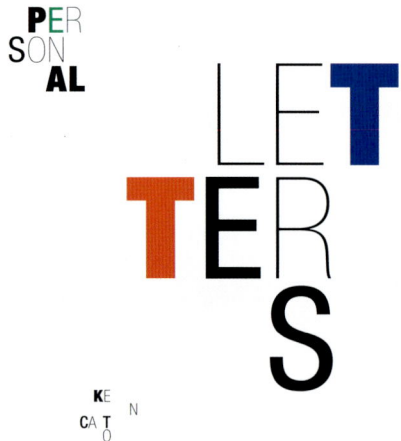

'Personal Letters' is a book that explores the way in which designers use the different characteristics of individual letters as a key component in design projects

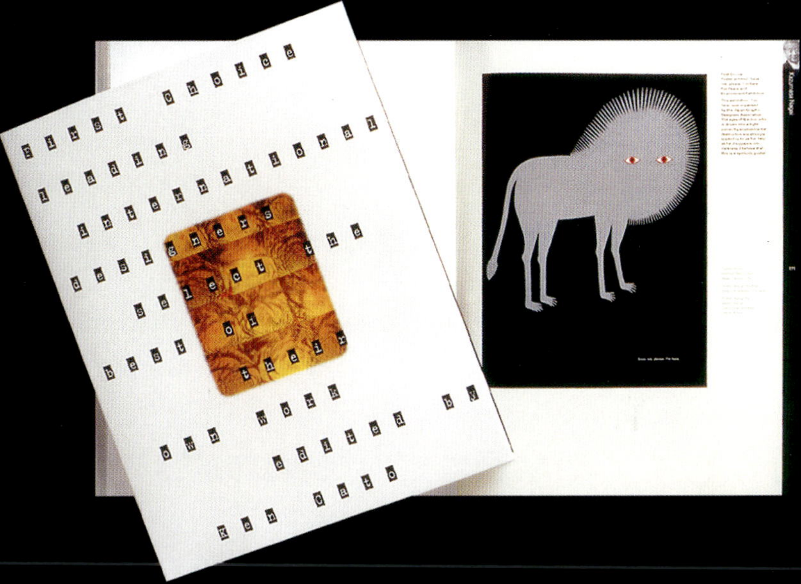

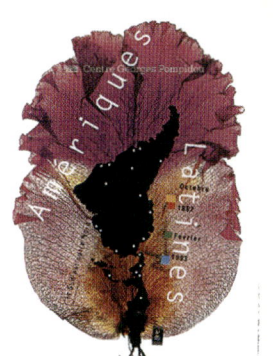

Covers and editorial spreads for 'Edge' magazine

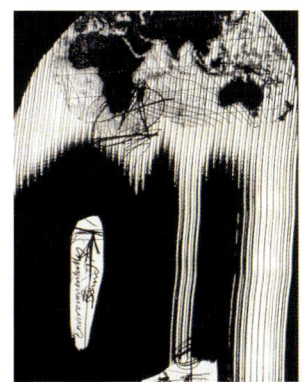

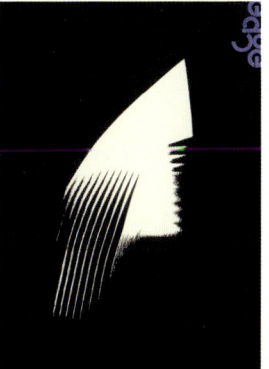

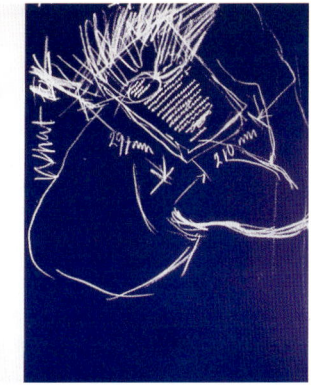

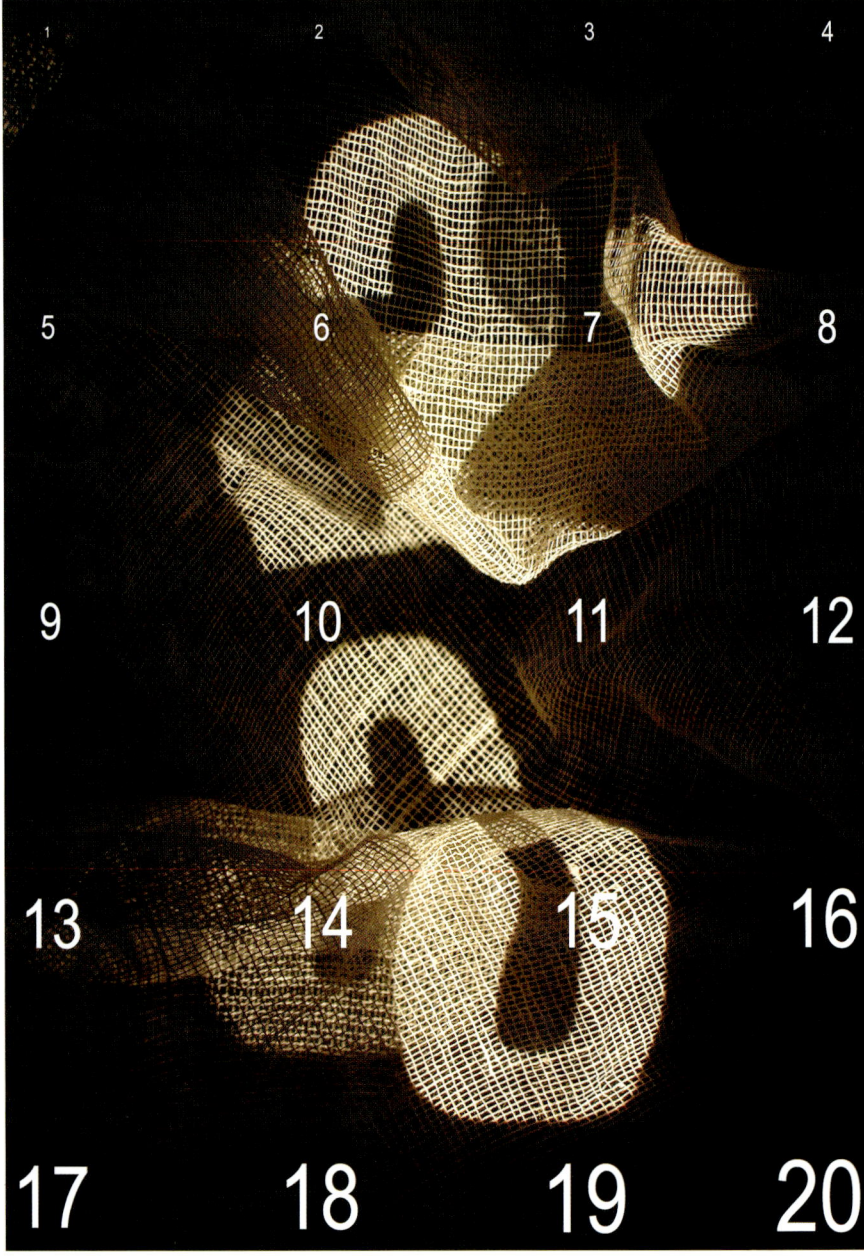

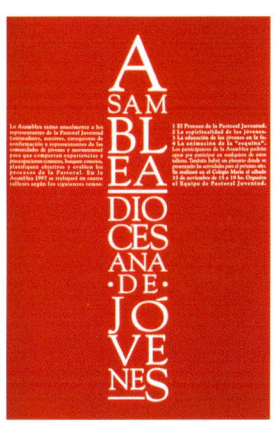

The best known symbol of Christianity was graphically restated on a series of posters to communicate specific events in a contemporary way to youth groups of the Diocese in San Isidro, Argentina Opposite page: Poster celebrating the 20th Anniversary of the Bruno Biennale

Promotional material for Urbane Publicity, a Japanese photographic studio

A graphic treatment of the symbol for Te Papa, New Zealand's national museum, features prominently in the organisation's corporate literature

Two posters for Japan's DDD Gallery invitational poster exhibition

Opposite page: The fourth poster for the annual AGIdeas international design conference

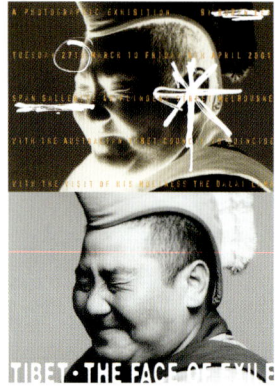

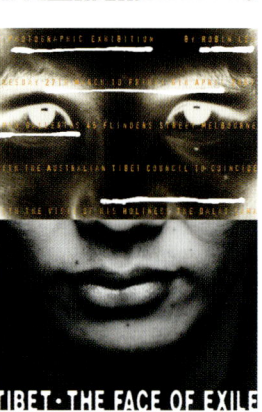

A series of posters to promote a photographic exhibition by Robyn Lea, and a poster for the Sydney 2000 Olympic Games

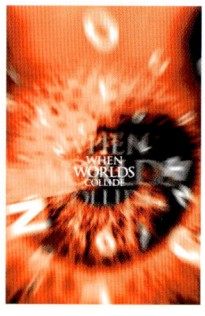

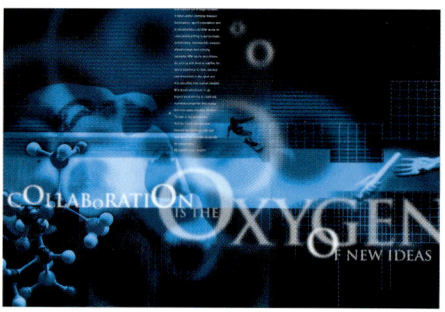

A promotional brochure for Sportsworld Media Group

Opposite page: Covers for *The Rocker*, a staff magazine produced for the Bank of New Zealand

Examining the third dimension

Right: At World Expo '88 held in Brisbane, Australia, the theme of time was represented at ground level by a series of sculptures that depict the measurement of time. Neon pieces including metronomes, hourglasses and time-lines, continue the theme
Opposite: Developed in Argentina, these commissioned dimensional papers became the graphic elements of a promotional calendar and wine label

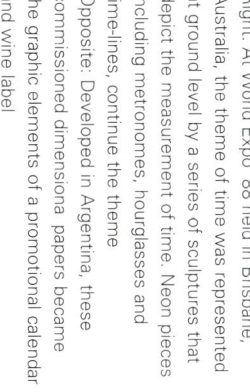

Below: Signage and architectural graphics programme for BHP Petroleum Australia
Following pages: The main gathering point at World Expo '88 was called Time Square. Approximately 7.5 kilometres of neon lighting traversed the ceiling of this area, colouring the quadrants to depict the passing of time through the four seasons of the year

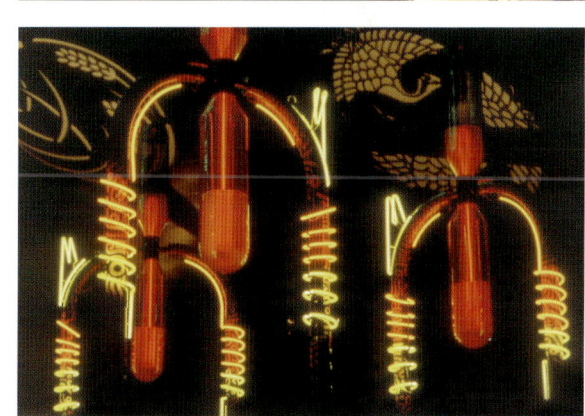

Opposite page: Sculptures for the City of Melbourne's 1996 Olympic Games Bid

Forecourt sculptures for the Westmead Children's Hospital

you are invited to participate in the australian launch of the Laminex colour spectrum

colours that respond to your specifications

the launch will reveal our new colour range together with other new products and future developments from Laminex Industries

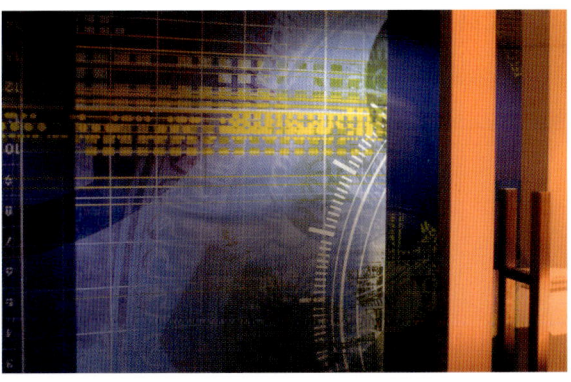

Opposite page: Poster and exhibition sculptures to launch a new range of products for Laminex Industries

Symbol and environmental graphics for the National Australia Bank's e-commerce division

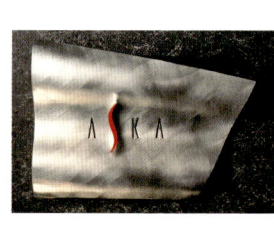

Architectural graphics and signage for Pharaoh Pub and Karaoke Bar, Acacia Hotel Indonesia; Raffles Grill and Empire Cafe, Raffles Hotel Singapore; and Aska, Hyatt Regency in Johor Bahru

Opposite page: The Borneo Pub, architectural graphics for the Dusit Inn Balikpapan in Indonesia, and the Hyatt Regency Surabaya

Architectural graphics and signage programme for Melbourne Sports and Aquatic Centre

Components of the identity programme for the national airline of Argentina, Aerolíneas Argentinas

The Broader Visual Language for Aerolineas Argentinas embraced all aspects of the airline's resources

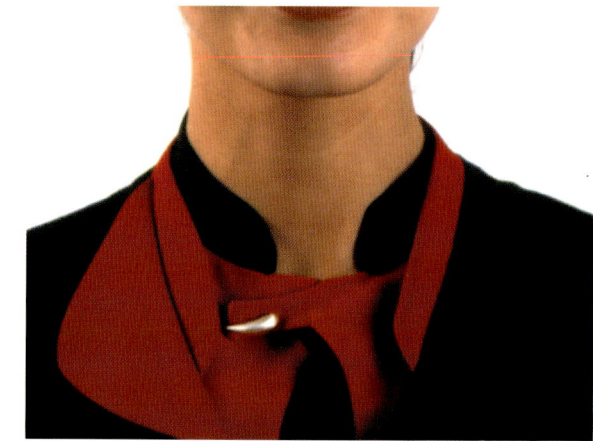

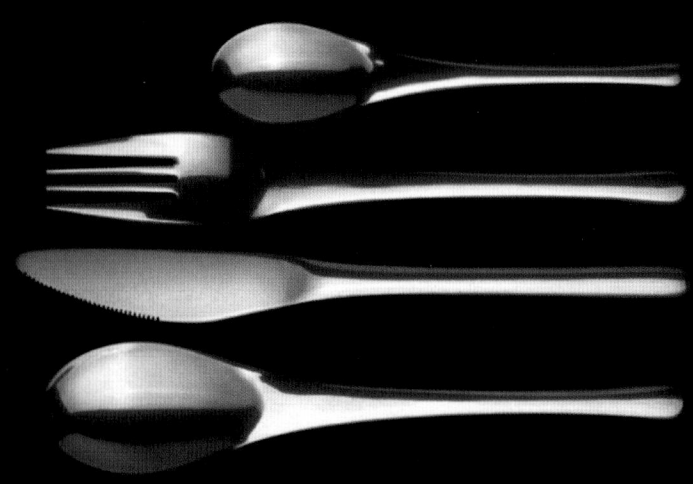

Packaging and wall graphics for Te Papa,
New Zealand's national museum

To celebrate the 70th anniversary of the
David Jones department store, photographs from
seven decades of women's fashion were used
to cover every window of the store

Carry bags for Andersons (homewares stores), Museum of Victoria's Scienceworks, Starfish (retail fashion) and Rowlands at Como (food court)

Ceiling for the underground walkway at Mexico's Monterrey Airport designed in collaboration with Gabriela Rodriguez

# NAIL LACQUER

BY POPPY

The brand identity and packaging system for Poppy cosmetics

Graphics and packaging for James Reyne's compact disc 'Design for Living'. The album's title song dealt with two opposite living environments and their social implications

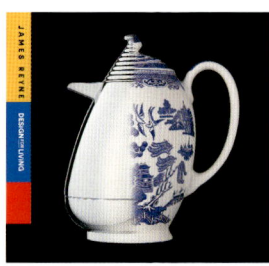

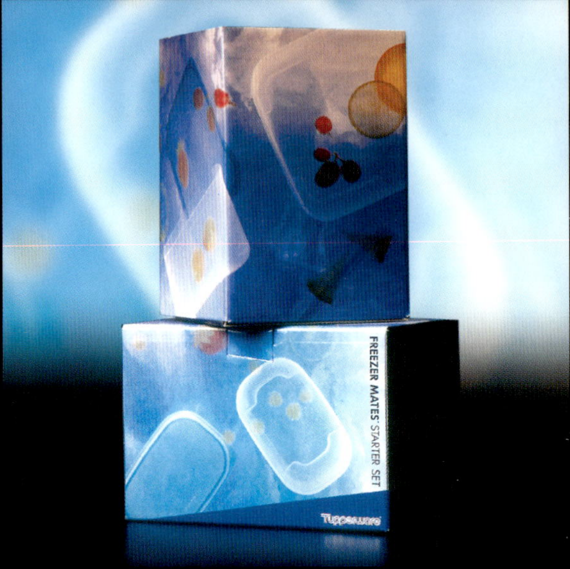

FREEZER MATES STARTER SET
Tupperware

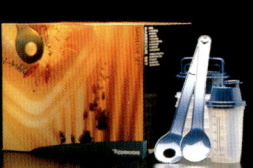

Corporate print and promotional material for Adam Ellis, a New Zealand-based environmental designer
Opposite page: Tupperware packaging

Selected examples from the home-branded packaging programme for Woolworths, Australia's leading supermarket chain

A new dessert wine from San Pedro Vineyards in Chile gave opportunity for a dramatic three dimensional butterfly packaging concept

Pioneering winemakers T'Gallant on the Mornington Peninsula have embraced innovative and bold packaging to accompany their new and experimental wine styles. Holystone and Demi Vache are shown here, and examples on the following two pages, show more products from this Australian winery

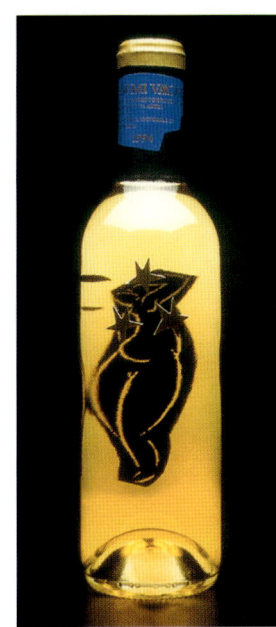

The packaging for KWC wines features artwork created during the year of vintage

Wine packaging and trademarks for Peerick, Stefano Lubiana Osborns and Caledonia Australis vineyards

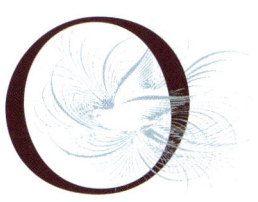

Wine packaging and trademarks for Boyntons, Prospero and Tarrawarra Tin Cows wineries

Within the fourth dimension

Symbol for the Seven Network, a leading Australian television network, conveys its origins in the animated sequences

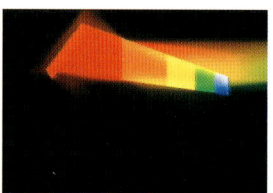
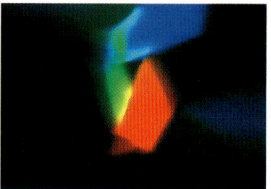

Opposite page: The symbol is brought to life as a screen saver for the company's workstations

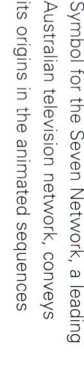

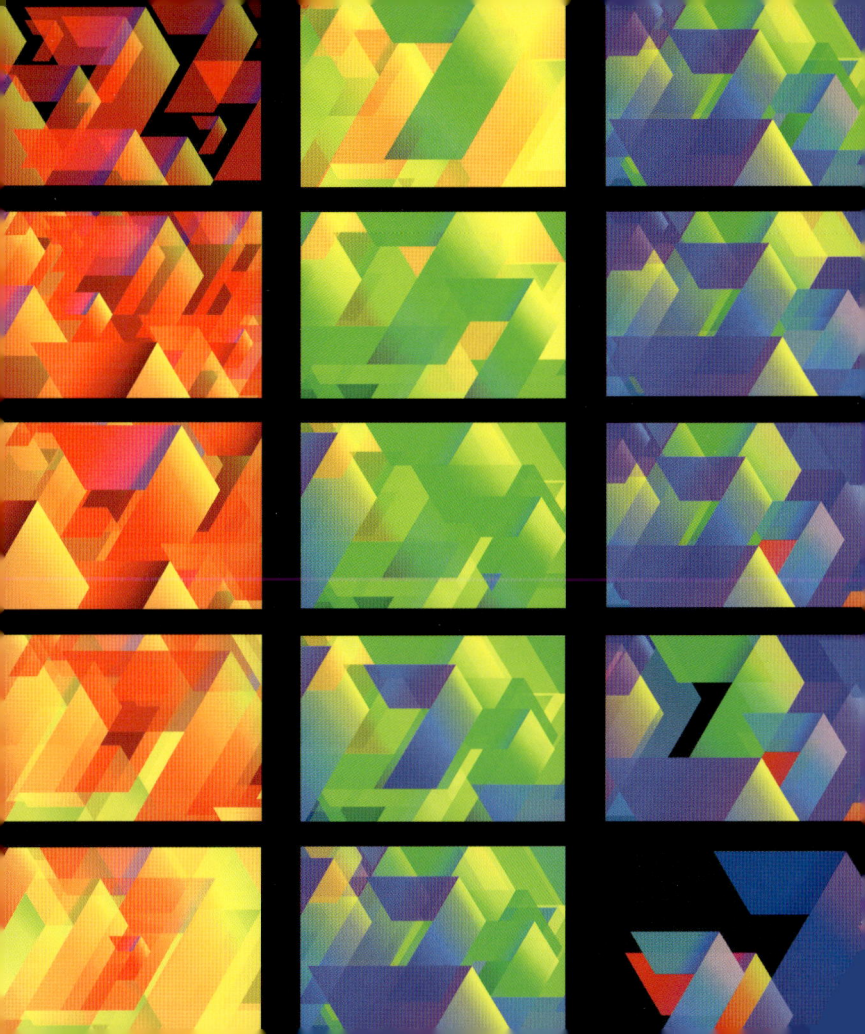

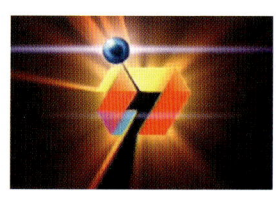

Trademark and animation sequences for i7 and Seven Productions

106

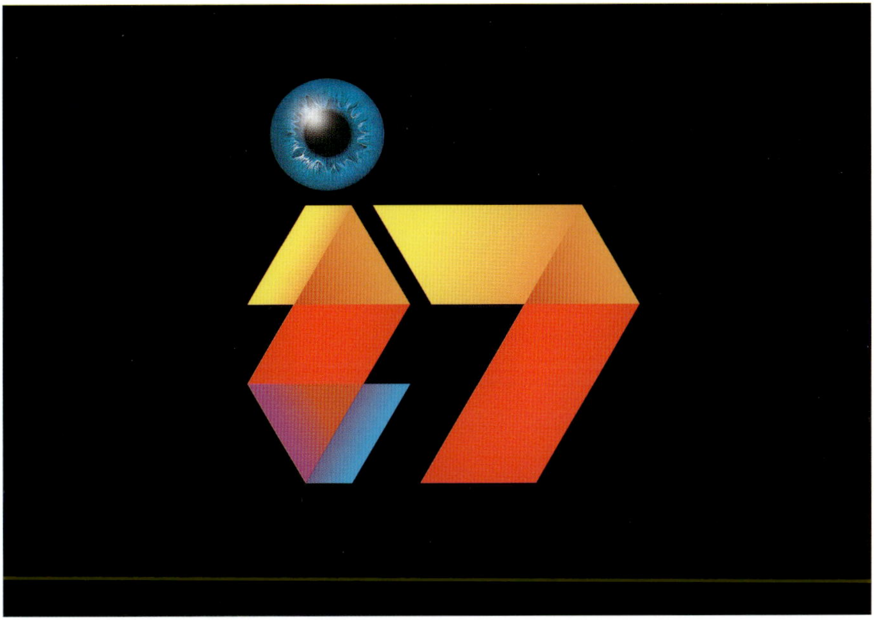

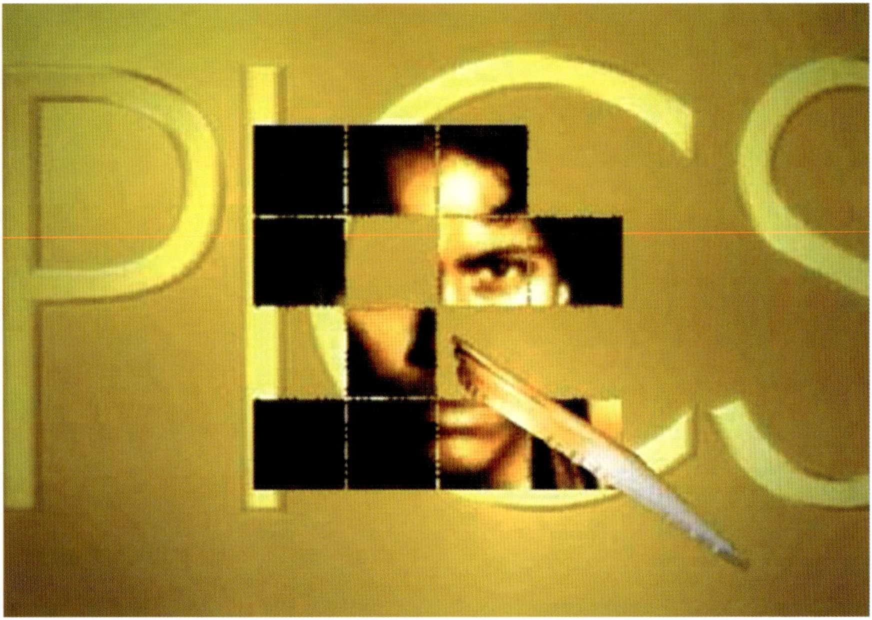

Animated graphics for C7, the Seven Network's cable sports channel

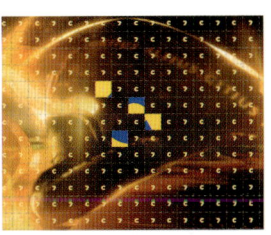
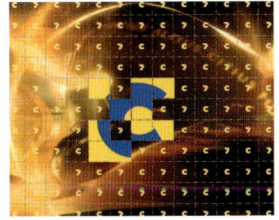
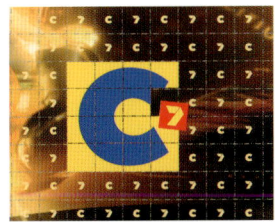
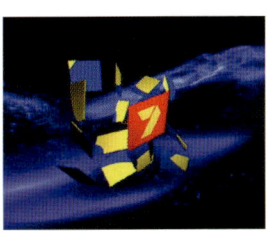
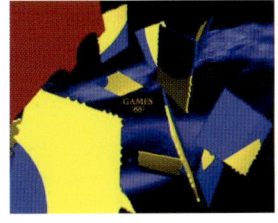
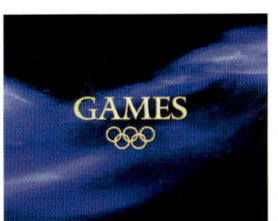

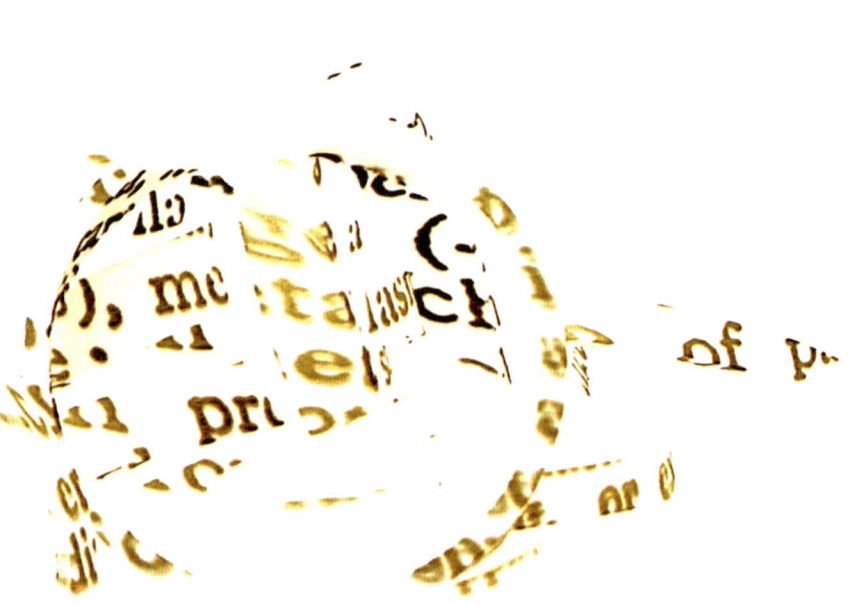

This spread and the next show experimental animated sequences from 'Metaplasia', a work related to the transition of typographical elements

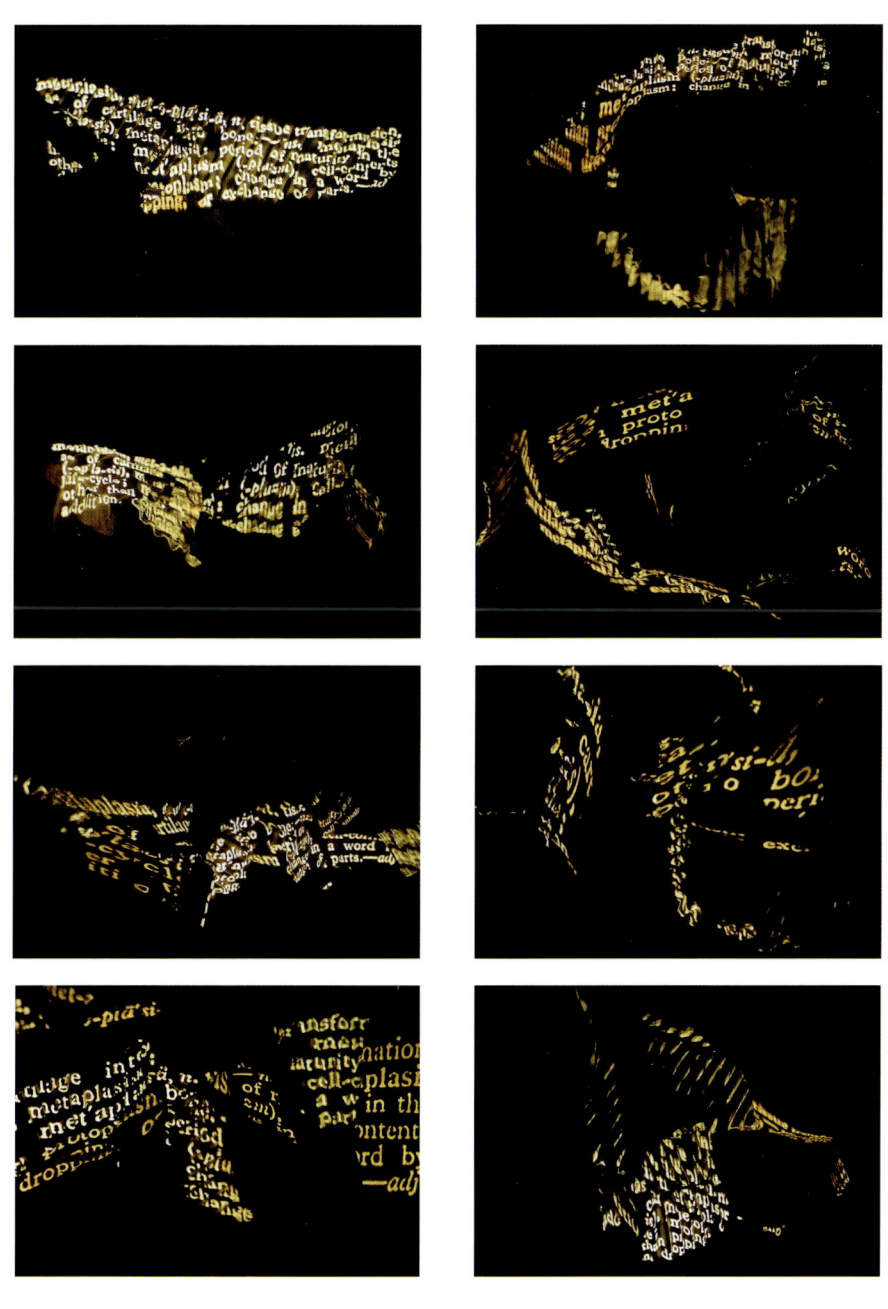

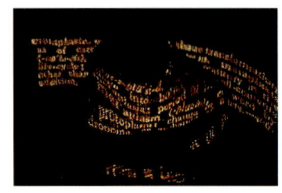

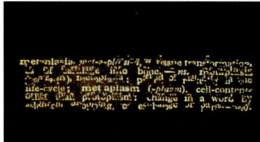

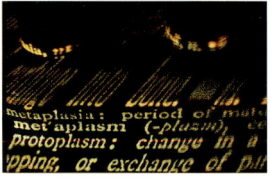

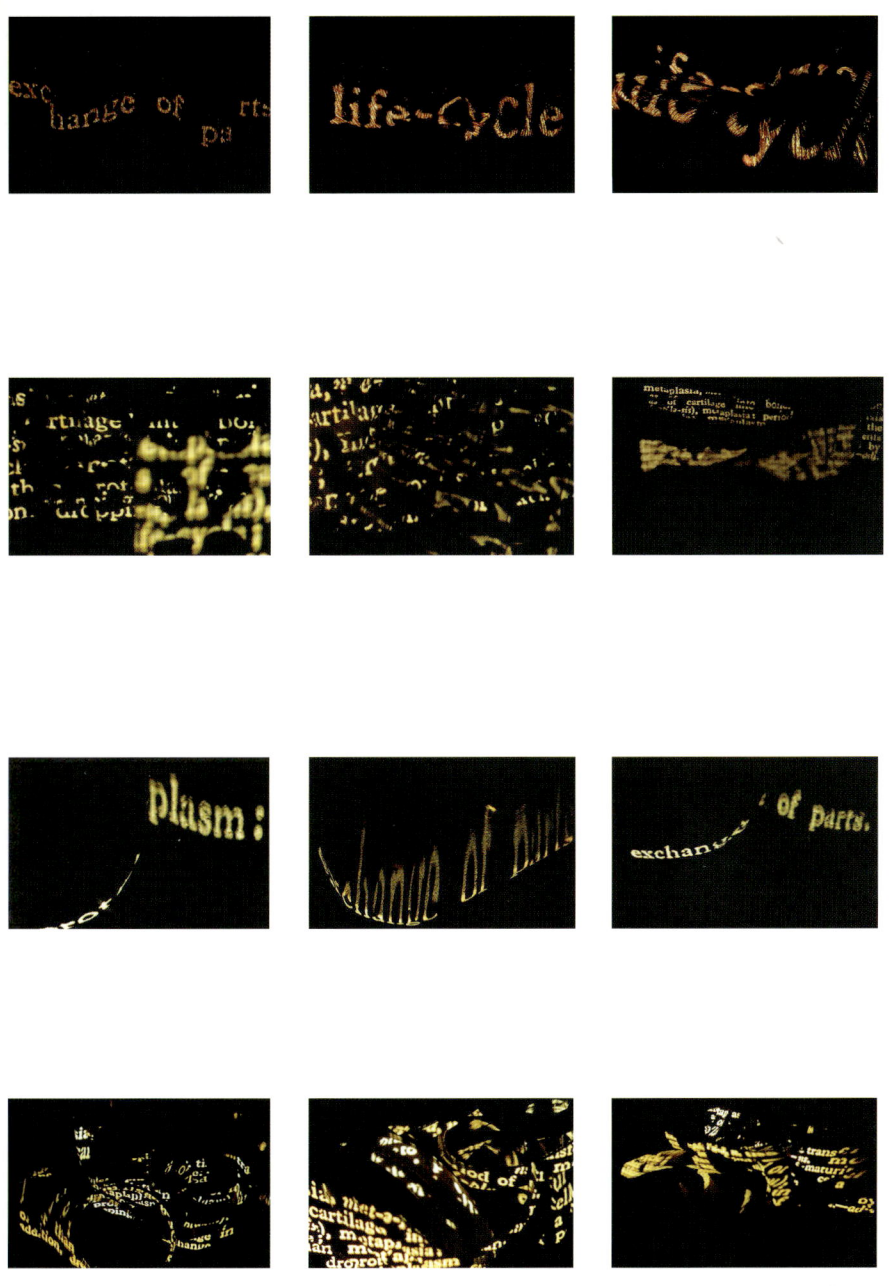

Under the Time Square ceiling at World Expo 88, a videotape reinforced the theme of time. These frames show images depicting the human life cycle in parallel with the passing of the four seasons

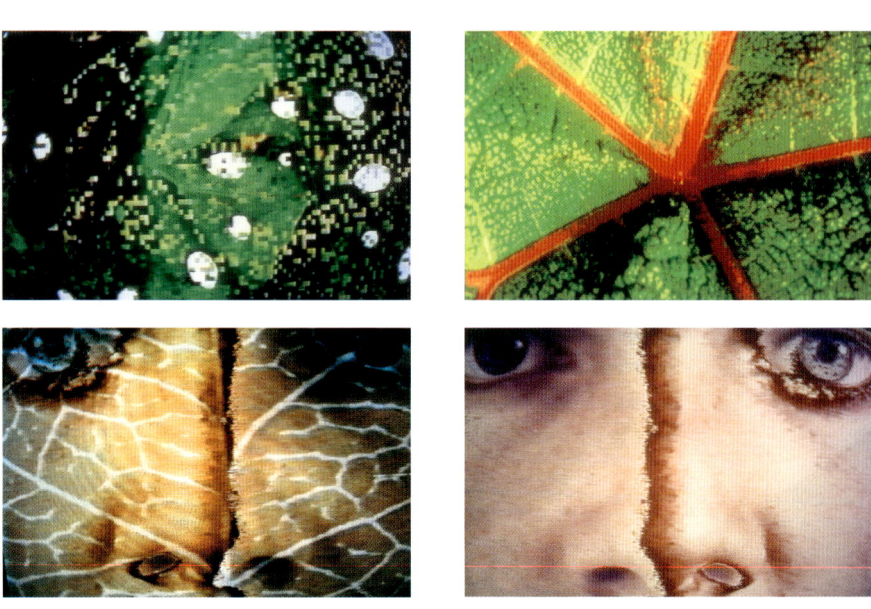

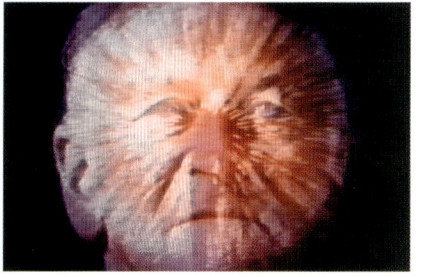 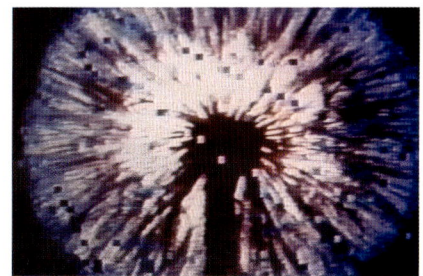

Frames of the corporate identity from the animated graphics for Deep Fire, an independent film and television production company
Opposite page: Identity programme and animation stills for Cinemedia, a government organisation that assists the production, distribution and exhibition of screen content and culture

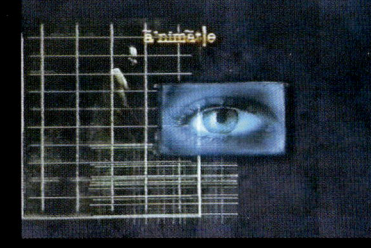
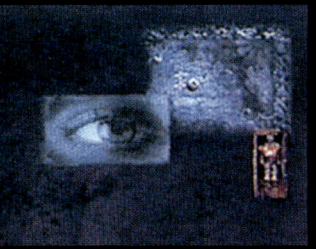
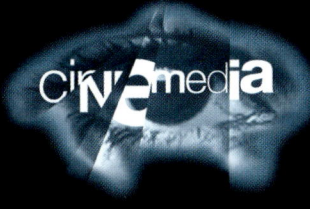
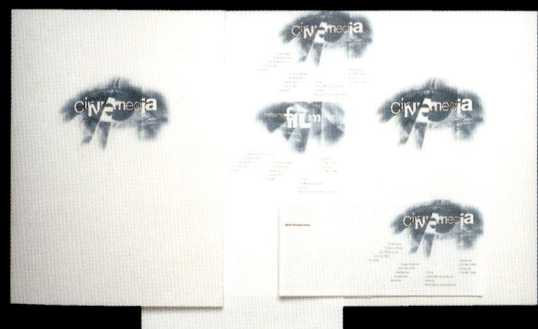

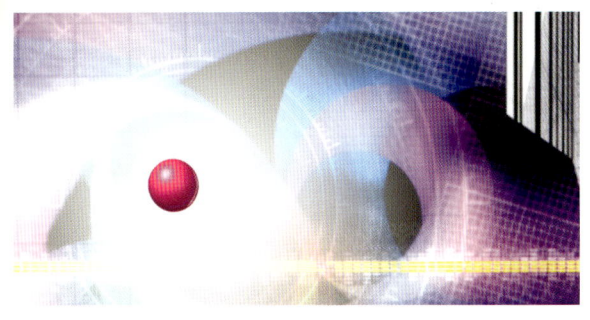

Trademark and animated graphics for the National Australia Bank's e-commerce division

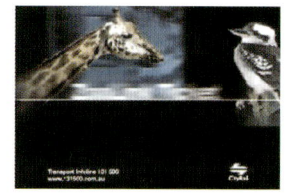
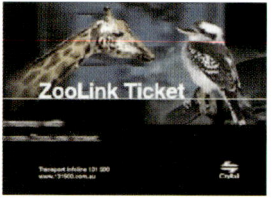

Animated station posters for CityRail, one the world's largest commuter networks

**State Rail Authority of New South Wales**
1999-2000 Annual Report

StateRail

A logotype and animated figure form the basis of an identity programme for the West Australian Ministry for Sport and Recreation, an initiative to promote community participation and achievement through physical activity

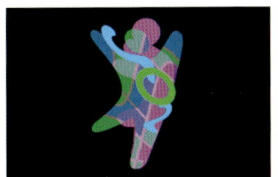

The personal viewer relationship with the regional television station provided an animated solution for the identity of the Prime television channel. The concept of 'me' and 'prime' came from within the organisation's name

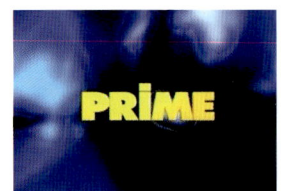

PRIME

ME

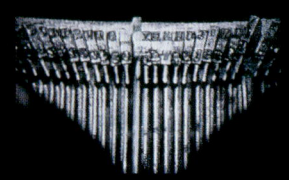

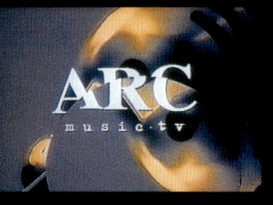

The identity programme was ideally suited to the development of a series of animated cable channel identity videos

# ARC
music·tv

design by thinking is always difficult